Inside the Mind of a Jewelry Designer

Inspiration, Passion and the Journey to Your Creative Self

MW00887672

Inside the Mind of a Jewelry Designer

Inspiration, Passion and the Journey to Your Creative Self

ISBN-13: 978-1481021586

ISBN-10: 1481021583

First Printing, 2012

Printed in the United States of America

Dedication

This book is dedicated to my Father who instilled in me the love of knowledge and the power of the written word and my Mother who shared with me her passion for art and creativity.

Additional Titles by Alene

"The Twin Cities New Age Directory"

(Out of Print)

Member Of

Arizona Art Alliance

Arizona Designer Craftsman (ADC)

Society of North American Goldsmiths (SNAG)

Featured In

Best of American Jewelry Artists, Volume III

Kennedy Publishing

Table of Contents

Section 1

Inside the Mind of a Jewelry Designer

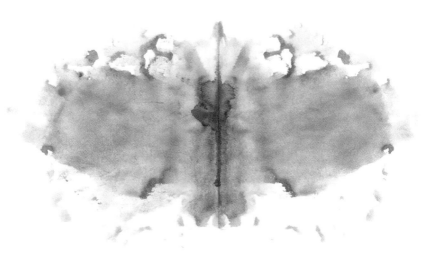

*"Someone may not remember what you
SAID but they will always remember
how you made them FEEL."*
Author Unknown

Inspiration, Passion and the Journey to Your
Creative Self

1

The Creative Mind of an Artist

The "Art" of Becoming An Artist

Any artist you speak with will likely tell you that they have no choice in creating their art, no matter the medium. They simply *must*. Creating art is not a choice like other careers; it is a "calling" that dominates our waking moments and sometimes our sleep – it's an obsession. Since becoming a jewelry designer and experiencing for myself the complete joy and passion that it provides me,

I have become fascinated with creativity and exploring inside the mind of a jewelry designer. And so, this book, yet another creative endeavor, was born. I've discovered that the creative process that it takes to design a piece of jewelry is much the same as the process that it takes to design a life of purpose – the life that I've created due, in large part, to what I've learned in the creative process.

I want to share my journey with you and give you the opportunity to experience this same joy and the absolute euphoria of living your passion and becoming the creative person you were meant to be.

What is Creativity?

To create is to produce something new and unique, from one's thoughts or imagination; something of value that did not exist previously.

Creative self-expression is empowering. As humans, we can be moved by a work of art and become emotional just being in its presence. Designing and creating can provide emotional and physical healing and personal self-growth in ways that few other forms of therapy and self-improvement can. So, allow your self-expression to take you on a magnificent journey – one that will alter who you are forever!

Your Creative Personality

Why are some people more creative than others? There are characteristics of the creative mind. As designers, we are non-conforming by nature. We tend to be more flexible than others and have a natural curiosity, shifting easily from one problem or project to another. We are likeable, happy, sensual, sexually curious, impulsive, and self-reliant and have high energy for seeking pleasure. In short, we enjoy life!

We crave excitement and enjoy optimistic people who are also impulsive and curious, but we sometimes avoid getting "too deep" and tend to avoid difficult discussions, preferring instead to direct our introspective tendencies toward our passion and designs. We do not tolerate boredom well and are not prone to routine – who else besides an artist can understand the need to work on a piece until three in the morning? Here then, are more fascinating aspects of the creative personality:

The Need for Solitude

We are all familiar with the (romantic!) image of the artist in the throes of creativity: The painter working feverishly in his Paris loft through the night - the writer driving through the snowstorm in the dead of winter to reach his cabin in the woods so he can be alone in his thoughts and write. The jewelry designer, poised over her workbench, deep in thought. Designers often engage in self-imposed isolation. For most designers, creativity flourishes in solitude. We reach inside ourselves to find the truth in our work.

Art and Risk Taking

An artist has the ability to communicate emotion non-verbally through some means of creativity. The process, intuitive to most artists, includes integrating a vision with the process of making it come to life. Creativity is risk. Anytime you step outside yourself and risk judgment from others, you are vulnerable. Creating art is a true baring of one's soul! Anais Nin, a French-Cuban writer whose journals spanned over 60 years wrote *"And the day came, when the risk to remain tight in a bud was more painful than the risk it took to blossom."*

Passion and Your Need to Create

Why must we, as designers, create? Why do we feel this passion? This obsession? The creative mind is different – this is clear. Science has found that creative people have a higher level of dopamine in the brain. Dopamine is a chemical found in the mesolimbic pathway, which is responsible for reward-driven behaviors like pleasure, euphoria, motor function, compulsion, spontaneity, curiosity and preservation.

Dopamine plays a major role in the brain system. If you have a creative personality, you have a higher propensity to experience feelings of enjoyment and reinforcement when dopamine is released.

2

Creating a Passionate Life

"Creativity is inventing, experimenting, growing,
taking risks, breaking rules,
making mistakes, and having fun."
Mary Lou Cook

My evolution to designer and artist has taken a circuitous and wondrous route; one in which I have learned so much more than I ever could have imagined!

In looking back at the journey to *my* creative self, I realize that the flow of this journey very much mimics the process that I use in creating a new design. My journey – my *life* – and finding my passion began taking shape as the most magnificent piece of art that I have created and I am pleased to share that with you, my readers. If we are open to change and growth, if we are listening with an open heart, a life of passion is ours to claim.

I've made the decision – which is really out of my hands at any rate – to pursue my passion and invite you to pursue yours; to evolve into the passionate, creative person *you* were born to be!

Change is sometimes hard. Sometimes we hold onto old feelings about ourselves. We listen to worn out scripts (*"I'm not creative ..." "I can't ..." I'm not good enough"*) out of habit. New ways of thinking – and being – do not always come easily because we are really not sure that if we *do* change, this change will produce the results we desire.

Habit is a choice though, and perhaps like you, I was ready to transition *away* from the things that were no longer working – and *towards* a more complete sense of myself.

Change ultimately is all we have. No matter how hard we try to control this change, people around us evolve, grow older, move away and die. Our jobs change, our family changes and of course we cannot help but grow and become different ourselves with each passing day.. Design and my willingness to jump in and 'change' has inspired an entirely new life for me. Let me share with you my journey towards discovering my creativity and passion.

In Section 2, I share with you, eight steps in the creative process when designing art of *any* kind:

1. Observation

2. Inspiration

3. Concept

4. Creation

5. Perspective

6. Narrative

7. Emotion; and

8. Motivation

I share with you how these design steps have inspired me to make significant changes in my life as an artist, wife, sister, friend, and business owner. In Section 3, we will talk about how you can do the same through exercises specifically designed to help you gain awareness and insight and to begin your own creative journey. The insight I've gained from each of these steps has been priceless, for, as in a great design, each is necessary for true growth. There are no shortcuts, but each holds the potential for magnificent growth and wisdom. Enjoy!

Inside the Mind of a
Jewelry Designer

Section 2

The "Art" of Becoming an Artist
My Creative Journey

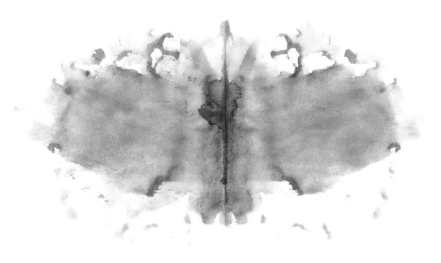

*"And the day came, when the risk to remain
tight in a bud was more pain than the risk it
took to blossom."*
Anais Nin

Inside the Mind of a
Jewelry Designer

3

Observation

*The process of observing significant details
carefully to gain information.*

An artist's mind is open, searching, *thirsty*, for inspiration. He or she has a heightened sense of observation; but may be entirely unaware that they are observing. Where others see a sunset and look away, an artist drinks in the brilliant hues of gold, orange, red. She truly "sees" the blues and purples that others cannot. Shapes and forms magically appear and a mental note is recorded: *"I* must *remember that for my design!"* A designer and artist notices that which others might consider banal and uninteresting: Patterns formed by the shadow of a fence perhaps, or the wood grains staining a lovely piece of mahogany flooring. The mind is constantly active, intrigued, and inspired by even the simplest of everyday occurrences and observations. In short, the artist finds b*eauty* in the world!

Observation & My Creative Journey

The influence of design in my creative journey has opened me – I truly *see* and gain insight into more than I ever could have imagined. Design, like life, demands observational skills. We must learn to see the minute details of everyday life in order to grow. In observing my life to this point, I realized a major influence of my own journey to my creative self, leading me to the realization that I *craved* change. In my personal life, I felt as if I was a human "doing" rather than a human "being." In my marketing career, I developed ideas and proposals on demand and while I found my work creative and inspiring most of the time, I also found myself "doing" to simply meet deadlines.

Opening myself to the possibilities enabled me to begin honing my observation skills. Mindfulness is key to accepting that which is working in our lives, and being open to the possibility of a more fulfilling life. I did not realize it at the time but the stage was being set for true change in my life; I was simply waiting for the moment to become – *inspired!*

In Section 3, I share with you some techniques that help you hone your observational skills and gain awareness, both of that around you as well as change that you may want to occur in your life to enhance your design and help you on your creative journey.

4

Inspiration

Mental stimulation to do
something creative.

Freud said, *"When inspiration doesn't come to me, I go half-way to meet it."* The literal translation of inspiration means to "breathe into." To inspire is to infuse some idea or purpose – to experience an awakening. As an artist and designer, I gain inspiration from many sources.

Historically, inspiration "visited" an artist in the form of a muse bestowing artistic gifts from above – "divine inspiration." In the early 1900s, however, the concept of creativity changed from the perspective as something outside of us (and thus, more difficult to access) to that produced from within (and so, more accessible, more easily developed). A new concept of inspiration posited that our unconscious is actually the source of our creativity.

Left-Brain – Right Brain

Is there truth to the theory that we possess dominant charac-teristics on either the left or right hemisphere of our brain that provides a clue into the potential for our creativity? Scientists studying the source of creativity have found through research that indeed, that there *is* a difference in how our brains function and control our bodies, based on left or right hemisphere dominance. Let's take a look at some of the characteristics found in the left and right hemisphere:

Left Hemisphere Dominant

The person with dominance on this side is believed to be more rational, analytical, cautious and in control of their feelings. They are comfortable with planning, structure and rules leading to better performance in subjects such as math and science. They prefer to communicate via talking or writing.

Right-Hemisphere Dominant

The person with right brain dominance is more intuitive and feeling. They are fluid, spontaneous, and are free with their feeling and are often labeled "dreamers". They prefer to communicate via objects and materials and of course, make great artists!

How does this affect your art? Well, you may well recognize yourself as being "right-brain" dominant, or you wouldn't have been interested in this book in the first place! And it is just as

likely that you identify with certain aspects of "left-brain" dominance as well. You may feel as if it you are totally creative
and abstract (something that also appeals visually more to the
"right-brain") but still need an orderly, organized workspace in
which to work (something that appeals to the "left-brain" dominant person). An important distinction of left-brain versus
right-brain in terms of your art, is that the left-brain typically
sees the detail in a piece and works their way outward to view
the whole, whereas the right-brain dominant person sees the
entire piece as a whole and then works their way inward to no-
tice details. It is felt that this distinction provides the ability to
"see" a piece in its totality, in our minds, even before it's created – and figure out the details during the creative process.

Inspiration & My Creative Journey

Inspiration comes to me at unlikely times; and I let it flow. I
may spot a sculpture or wall hanging that immediately sparks
the concept for a new jewelry design, or even a collection. A
blush of color may catch my eye. I feel drawn to it and am in-
stantly designing and creating my next piece in my mind;
inspired to use the color! Design demands inspiration – first
we observe that which is around us, then we are inspired to
create (more about that in a moment).

Inside the Mind of a
Jewelry Designer

My inspirational moment in my journey to my creative self –
my door opening to change and a passionate life – was quite
unexpected! It was a moment in which a switch was "flipped"
and I suddenly became this new, more creative, more passionate, and more *alive*, version of me. Let me share with you
my "moment":

I am in my office, admiring a turquoise necklace that a co-
worker has created to duplicate a product produced by a well-
known jewelry sales company. Incredible! Suddenly I feel
compelled to create – I *have* to construct something just as
stunning. I have no choice but to trust these feelings and
simply go with them – let them move me forward to my next
step. Inundated with images of beads I have at home, rem-
nants from temporary ventures in amateur beading, I cannot
wait to begin digging through my stash – each bead more
beautiful than I remembered. I spend the next several days on
scouting trips to bead stores – each presenting me with more
stunning selections. I can hardly contain my enthusiasm!

Change comes when we are ready to embrace it and are open
to the possibilities it presents – and although my "moment"
seems innocuous, I am totally unprepared for the incredible
effect and amazing changes that I now know await me. Becoming an artist, and the freedom and joy that awaits in my

relationship with my husband, my career and personal growth, are in my future, but for now, I've found my moment – my purpose. I am OK with me – finally!

I've learned through design that inspiration abounds in life. I'm inspired literally every hour of every day. I create because it's impossible for me *not* to create. Inspiration surrounds me from the first thought of which material might best work in a piece to the absolute joy of experiencing the finished piece for the first time, to the image of my client who ultimately wears my designs. As in life, the beauty around me inspires my designs. Let me share with you some of the sources that I've found on my journey to my creative self – and to show you my very first silver piece!

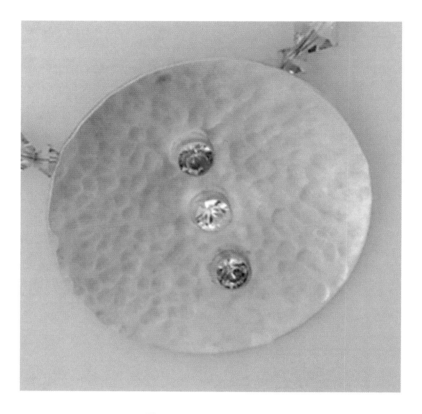

Figure 1: My First Piece!

Training & Workshops

Dream vacations still include a week on the beach or hiking for several days (for inspiration, fun and exercise!), but now one of my dream vacations is to attend an intensive jewelry retreat or workshop. A workshop would not have made the top 30 list ten years ago! I love taking classes and workshops to develop my skills. In the beginning of my career, I took every class available – every chance I got. Some classes are so exciting that I come home filled with even *more* directions in which to take my designs and, while I learn something from every class I've taken, some techniques just don't give me that "goose bump" effect I seek. I admire the skill it takes to create unique designs using these amazing techniques, but I instinctively know that I have to find my *own* design aesthetic by eliminating certain options and ~~by~~ choosing those techniques that speak to me personally.

Gemstones

Gemstones are truly inspiring, not only in their beauty but also in the mythology that surrounds them and the powers that they bestow on the wearer. In a later chapter, I look at the mythology surrounding these stunning stones and include a piece from my collection with the design process used in its creation.

Trade Shows & Events

I love finding the *perfect* gemstone for my designs and each year I attend the Tucson Gem show for exactly that reason.

The Tucson Gem Show (only 1 ½ hours from my home) is the largest gem show in the world. Each year in January and February, virtually every hotel and convention venue in Tucson is filled with gems, tools, rocks and much more. Many of the shows are open only to the wholesale trade but there are several that cater to the casual buyer looking for treasures for his or her personal use. It is the most fun a jeweler can have away from her own jewelry bench!

This year I found some incredible Malachite and Red Creek Jasper gemstones. Last year, I found stunning Picture Jasper and Rhodochrosite. I have included the pieces in their raw form along with the finished piece – you simply don't know what you're going to find! I've included some of the pieces, and a finished pendant, that I found at the show on the following page.

Figure 2: Pieces from the Tucson Gem Show

My Clients

While I design for myself first, it is also important as a designer, to know your client and to gain inspiration from her. Feedback from clients and fans reaffirm that my designs reflect my passion. I love knowing that my customer feels joy when wearing my design!

Who *is* my client? She is independent, feels empowered and accepts who she is. She loves feeling feminine and stylish. She is attracted to artisan jewelry that shows off her true essence and passion for life. And she is approachable; she's a woman others want to get to know and call "Friend."

My Final Design

Once my design is completed, I feel complete joy! If along the way my design isn't "flowing", I've learned to stop, take a break, and revisit it later. Taking a break like this gives me the opportunity to see the design through fresher eyes. Often when I see the design again, it speaks to me and I know it comes from my passion. And just as often, I know the design just is not right; simply put: It's not *me*. Then I can make adjustments or start over. This part of the process is very important. I want each piece, each design, to reflect my vision and come from my heart.

5

Concept

An abstract idea; a notion –
a plan or intention.

The influence of design on my abilities to conceptualize my creative journey – and the life that *I* want to create – is invaluable. Design demands a concept: We observe, we become inspired, and *then* we conceptualize how to make that which has inspired us, into reality. Developing a concept is the next critical step in the creative process and entails feeling and *being* present at all times. It is during this step that I ask myself the question *"I wonder …?"* "I wonder what happens if I combine these two elements?" "I wonder how to make this piece look like what I'm envisioning?" "I wonder what happens if I do *"this*?"

Conceptualizing the life I want has been a true joy since becoming a designer. Aren't we *all* designers, after all, of our own lives? Shouldn't we all feel that passion, that connection, to our family, our work – and especially to our lovers – that we feel for the design process?

Conceptualizing a *more* passionate, *more* fulfilling life is seam-less using the disciplines I've learned as a designer.

Concept & My Creative Journey

Developing a concept for a piece – the evolution of the design taking shape is the most fun! This process spans the entire creation of the piece of course, and is driven forward signifi-cantly in the concept phase. The vision comes to me initially, shifting somewhat as the piece progresses and when my vi-sion and the progression of my design are in sync – it's pure magic! In Section 3, I'll show you how you can develop a con-cept based on the knowledge you have to this point: Your observations and the inspiration you've gained.

6

Creation

*The process of bringing something into
existence, especially something of artistic talent.*

Design demands of course, the ability to create. We have observed that which is around us, which has inspired us to conceptualize something new – to create! My creative process is an obsession – a magnificent obsession! It is here that I move from *"I wonder ..."* to *"I can ..."!* In creating custom designed pieces specifically for my female family members (and their wonderfully unique personalities!) one Christmas, my niece's husband asked, *"How do you think of all these different designs?"* "I can't *NOT* think of them," I replied. "My head is constantly filled with concepts, ideas, colors, forms, textures. It never turns off!"

The process of creating my jewelry has taught me much about life.

Creating & My "Creative" Journey

Everything is a learning experience and I have had lots of them! Precision is vital in creating a design; the components must fit and be finished well, to complete a stunning look. Early on, when I was just beginning metalwork, I can remember soldering a bezel for a gemstone cabochon. This means the backside is flat so it can be mounted easier into the bezel (the sterling silver "frame" around the stone). I had completed the bezel, finished it nicely, and then soldered it to the backing. I was so proud of myself for getting this step done properly – except that I had soldered the bezel upside down; the flat side of the stone would actually be the part that shows! Not only would this be unattractive, but also it would be impractical since the 'bumpy' side of the gemstone won't fit on a flat surface. I had to scrap this and start over completely.

My lesson from this particular "mistake"? If I had taken the time to fit the stone into the bezel one more time before soldering to the backing, I would have caught this error easily.

Another project I envisioned involved adding a gemstone to one of my copper cuff creations. I was having trouble though, getting the solder to work well against the copper because it has to be completely free of any oxidation for this to work.

Silver solder is difficult to turn copper colored to help it blend. I had just been experimenting with riveting, which is hammering a sterling nail to connect two sides when I came up with the idea to design a smaller sterling piece, add the gemstone to the silver and rivet it to the cuff – and the mixed metal, gemstone cuff was born! I *love* the result, which has transformed into something even *more* stunning than its initial design.

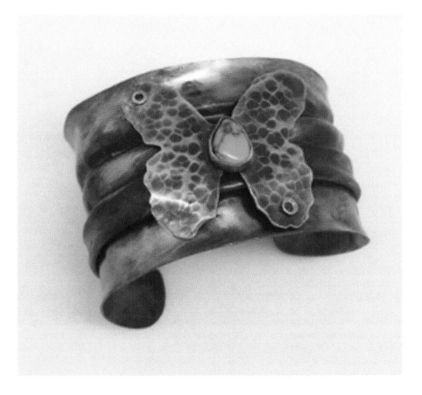

Figure 3: *Be Transformed* Copper, Sterling & Turquoise Butterfly Copper Cuff

Another design that became a "happy accident" was a set of malachite earrings for which I had purchased a gemstone cut so that it came to a point on one side. I decided to put the pointed side towards the bottom of the earring and while sol-dering the bezel to the backing, a tiny part of the bezel at the point melted because I had the torch too hot for the project.

After a few choice words (!) and time to feel sorry for myself, I calmed down and looked at the imperfection. Suddenly I could envision the bezel tapering down towards the point creating a unique design element.

So I set about filing away at the rest of the components to cre-ate this new look. The earrings are now in my personal collection and had I not made this mistake, I would not have discovered this new design! There are many such moments in the process of creating art: Sometimes a mistake can become a happy discovery of an entirely new design.

I had experimented with beading in the 90's, creating some pieces to wear, but jewelry design wasn't a serious pursuit at the time. I did not take the time to learn the skills required to create something of which I could be proud. I felt my work was not "good enough" anyway – since I did not consider my-self creative.

Design has taught me that living and creating in the moment means letting go of perfectionism – that I don't have to keep striving for perfection in order to be worthy, liked and appreciated. Once I discovered that mistakes aren't the end of the world and that good things can come from them, it freed me to be "in the flow" connecting both to others and to my design. Developing a well-thought out concept and carrying it through to creation didn't (and doesn't!) always happen just as I'd envisioned, but that's okay! An important part of the creative process is establishing a connection to the piece – this is critical. If I do not feel that connection, it's simply not meant to be. Every design I create carries a part of me in it. That is why I will not compromise on this process. In Section 3, I'll share exercises that I've designed that help you through the creative process, even when you've hit a block and feel as if no new ideas are opening up to you.

Inside the Mind of a
Jewelry Designer

7

Perspective

The communication and demonstration
of personal style.

The influence of design on my perspective – both within my designs, and my life in general has been exciting to see unfold. Design demands that I place my perspective, my own personal style, into the piece in order to provide a platform for a narrative and the emotion that I want to evoke in the wearer. Observation, inspiration, concept, and creation are given life by our perspective. Each one of us is unique as a designer and so is our perspective. Finding my personal style and layering it into my designs has been incredibly enriching and an ongoing process as I challenge myself creatively every time I sit at the jewelry bench.

Perspective & My Creative Journey

Putting my unique perspective on my jewelry is tremendously exciting! And, as I said, is ongoing process – an important life lesson. Are we ever truly *"done?"* While copper, sterling, and gemstones are key elements of my work, the techniques, patina, and finishes keep evolving as I learn, try, and experiment –

and take risks. My mind races constantly; my energy level is heightened when I think of design; ideas flow from me in every moment, of every day. When first beginning my design career, I found myself drawn to metals. My husband affectionately refers to me as the "Naked Jewelry Lady". Often I get up at the crack of dawn and head to the bench where he will find me working on a design. Putting on clothes would have wasted valuable design time after all!

Our perspective in our work builds as our skills and experiences develop. Let me share with you what I mean: I made my first pendant from sterling silver using techniques of forging, doming and soldering. Hooked! I had learned fold forming in a class that was the first step in my finding my "design voice" and – "hooked" again! I fell in love with the technique and use it often in my copper cuff collections, as in the piece on the following page.

**Figure 4: A Piece from My Copper Cuff Collection Featuring Copper,
Silver, and Brass**

This process was so much fun to do and I loved the results. I have shaped and formed copper in so many different directions, the collection just seemed to create itself. Now I add gemstones and sterling to many of the designs as well.

During my lifetime, I have frequented art fairs finding myself attracted to certain styles. If I have to define the style to which I am drawn, I would say it's Artisan: Unusual, one-of-a-kind, bold, but not overwhelming, finished well but not delicate or ornate: A design that makes me say *"Wow!"* Those years of looking at other designs have helped to shape my own design aesthetic.

8

Narrative

"Faith is taking the first step
even when you don't see the whole staircase."
Martin Luther King, Jr.

You are gifted visually as a designer, telling your story or narrative within your work. In fact, the term narrative jewelry refers to pieces that have meaning beyond their aesthetic making a statement through their visual imagery. Every piece of jewelry you create has a story, a narrative that makes it unique and an intimate part of you that is in everything you create. Blending your narrative with that of someone who wears and enjoys your jewelry, begins as your personal signature takes shape within the piece: How does this gem work with the metals? How are they related? What is the story behind this piece?

Narrative jewelry has gained recognition over the past 40 to 50 years as an art form. Jack Cunningham, a contemporary studio jeweler and Ph.D. from The Glasgow School of Art stated, *"… a piece of jewelry tells us something of the designer maker, who may otherwise remain quite anonymous."* We are more interested as artists, not in telling *our* narrative through the piece, but in telling, ultimately, the narrative of the wearer.

Your story – your narrative – *speaks* to someone.

Narrative & My Creative Journey

Design demands of us the "telling" of our story within our work. Our narrative frames the creative process that we are undertaking: Observation, inspiration, concept and finally the creation of the piece, in turn allows us to transfer our story to that of the person who ultimately wears our design. I have learned through my design process, my design narrative, that there is incredible value in sharing one's experiences with others. It is not an overstatement to say that the confidence and personal worth that I've experienced in my design work has made this book, and my ability to be open to others, possible.

I grew up in an alcoholic home that significantly affected my view of my self-worth and my relationships. Like many children of alcoholic homes, I sought approval constantly. I became the "good girl" learning the rules, being sure not to "rock the boat." From a child's perspective, this was necessary to keep the peace within my family. In a home such as this however, rules really do not apply. In fact, there are no rules – no "normal." And so, I made the decision early in my life, not to allow myself a moment of weakness and to provide for myself always. I would go as far as to say that this stance isolated me from others. Telling my story, if initially only through my designs, has allowed me to connect and develop a certain intimacy with my clients that I never could have imagined.

We all have a narrative that may or may not resonate with those around us, but if we don't tell it – if we don't take the risk to share, we'll never know.

Inside the Mind of a
Jewelry Designer

9

Emotion

*A state of mind or feeling like
love, anger, hate, joy, etc.*

The influence of design on my emotions is inspiring. Design *demands* emotion. A piece of art without emotion is an inanimate object. And so it is with a *life* devoid of emotion. We have observed, become inspired, developed a concept and created our design. We've introduced our perspective into our pieces and told our narrative – now we're ready to ensure that it contains the emotion we're intending to convey and that we possess the requisite desire to make it happen!

Emotion & My Creative Journey

Hiding my emotions became natural – a way of life. If I didn't let others know how I felt, I could avoid their rejection or wrath – I simply couldn't rely on their reactions. This strategy worked well for me, even as an adult, to a certain extent. For instance, in my career: There are upsides to be sure, in being a sales professional. I have the freedom to choose my clients and market niche and I experience a sense of fulfillment when I make the sale and provide the perfect idea and solution to

41

my clients. My ability to provide for myself kept food on my table, but I felt as if I was masking my true self. I loved the interaction with my clients but preferred to keep a professional distance. I worked to provide ideas necessary to please my client; always on a deadline and finding myself in the 'doing' mode often.

I had the sense that I shouldn't depend on *anyone* for my happiness and livelihood and carried it to the extreme. In fact, at times I made life decisions without consulting my husband. This distance extended into my reticence in initially accepting my creativity. While I grew up with a mother who loved the arts and created many craft pieces over the years, I never considered art or design as an outlet for which I was suited. In fact, I am not even able to draw a straight line or circle! While I dabbled in basic beading during the 90's, I never felt good enough to pursue it in depth. After all, I wasn't creative anyway. The journey to my creative self and the passion that I feel for design has breathed new life into my emotions and proved me wrong. It has changed my life! None of the emotional insight and awareness I've gained would be possible without my newfound passion for creating art which has proven the perfect outlet in which to pour these emotions – what a gift! The emotional floodgates opened and there is no closing them! I have no time for "not good enough." That concept is

flushed from my existence. Perfecting my craft and feeling –
no, experiencing – the connection with my art is all that matters. Other areas of my life have benefited from this emotional
paradigm shift as well:

My Marriage

My husband is one of those rare people who is fortunate to be
completely in touch with his emotions. In addition to his influence, I engaged in a guided program that a client
recommended and gained insight from spiritual work, allowing
me to become in touch with long-buried emotions.

Shortly after meeting my future husband, but prior to marrying,
I had several sessions with a psychologist. His assessment of
me was that I created an image of strength and confidence,
yet he saw fragility in me that I hid well. I understood what he
was saying – and agreed. I was unwilling though, to access
that fragile part of me at the risk of betraying my confident exterior. Originally, I looked for someone in a relationship who
processed life the same way I did. I was aware of my husband's emotional side, but viewed it as a weakness, rather
than a strength. I now realize how wrong I was and how much
more robust live can be when embracing your emotions. I
recognize and appreciate my husband's feelings much more

deeply and accept them, in turn, enhancing our relationship immeasurably.

Let me give you an example: Following this emotional "awakening" we attended the funeral services and burial of Tom, one of my husband's dearest and oldest friends. I knew Tom as well, but did not have the 40-year history and emotional attachment that he and my husband shared. While funerals are solemn occasions of course, I was able to maintain my "exterior" while showing the sadness I felt. During the burial however, I began cry uncontrollably. I truly *felt* the loss for my husband and for Tom's family. I felt connected to the event and the people attending. I believe the awakening of my design and the connectedness to others has provided me with a level of empathy that I was finally able to uncover within myself.

My husband's support in my creative process has absolutely been the most special part of this evolution in me. As you may imagine, I've changed significantly from the person he met and married 17 years ago, yet at each new crossroad, he's expressed total joy at my finding this passionate side of myself and offered his support. I inherited his top-of-the-line workbench that he had customized for his woodworking! Now, that is a sacrifice – willingly offered, and gratefully accepted – so I could pursue my passion.

Figure 5: My Prized Workbench With All the Necessary Tools Close At Hand!

Bill's gracious gift makes this space all the more special to me. During the hours that I am seated at this workbench, engrossed in my designs, the rest of the world ceases to exist. I am given the opportunity to just "be in the moment" and am grateful every day for the joy this bench provides.

Through this process, I have come to realize that the issues we experienced early on were in large part an attempt on my part to keep him from imposing his will on me and preventing me from "becoming." My irrational fear was that he would chip away at the parts of me that I had worked so hard to maintain. In many ways, this negated the intention of our marriage as a true partnership and served to widen the distance between us.

The release of emotions through my art has given me insight into my past *and* present. Including Bill in my life *and* my decisions is integral in allowing him to become a true partner and not the tyrant that I imagined him to be – again, a consequence of having grown up in an alcoholic home where nothing is as it seems. We now easily express our thoughts concerning our lives and I feel the co-creating and synergy that is so critical to any relationship. Clarifying expectations both for myself as a partner to the man whom I adore, as well as my expectations of him as a partner, has help us grow tremendously as a couple.

My Family

My sisters Marilyn and Melanie, (modeling one of my ring designs below) have maintained a good relationship with me over the years. While we shared a common upbringing it did not make us close emotionally, however, my connection to this passion called design has resulted in a strong emotional bond with both sisters.

We now share feelings more readily and I know we understand each other better. They both get excited about my
designs, wearing the pieces, sharing my site with friends and
offering suggestions to market my designs.

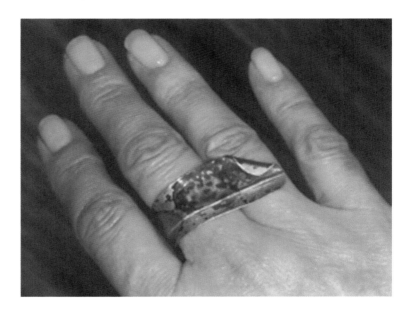

Figure 6: My Sister Mel's Princess Ring That I Designed
& Created For Her

Figure 7: Another Important Member of My Family;
Cici, My Kitty

My Marketing Career

My foray into design is felt *everywhere* in my day-to-day life! I
enjoy my marketing career, and am in awe at how it has transformed along with the rest of my life as I have integrated the
challenges I face in creating jewelry. Previously, I came into
the office pretty much expecting everyone to think the same
way I did: *"We're here to WORK! Do it my way and we will
get things done! No time for chit-chat!"* I did not recognize the
differences in personality and work processes as an opportuni-

ty to build a hugely effective team, but regarded it instead as a weakness.

Being more open emotionally allows me to encourage those around me to be themselves and trust that the job will get done, even if they do it their way! I appreciate the styles and differences of others and allow the synergy to produce even better results for me and my clients, co-workers, and employees. It has become the Win-Win scenario that I have always longed for, but never knew how to accomplish.

Inside the Mind of a
Jewelry Designer

10

Motivation

The desire to get something done!

It was Thomas A. Edison who said: *"Genius is one percent inspiration and ninety-nine percent perspiration."* And so it can be said for design as well! It is not enough to be inspired, we must act on that inspiration – and *that* takes motivation.

Motivation & My Creative Journey

Remaining focused continues to challenge me each day, with my goal being to remain focused and in charge of my activities so that I reach the potential that both my design and jewelry business offer. Design demands motivation. We may have been inspired by some observation that we made, developed a concept with our own unique perspective in which we could tell our narrative and added the emotion necessary to move others. And yet, without the motivation to actually create and to do everything necessary to place it on living person, our design has no life.

Motivation has never been an issue for me; I am self-directed and focused on my work. That carries through to my design work – in fact, if anything, I'm *more* motivated and driven when designing – some might say I'm consumed with design I love it so much! I have found this a common thread among design- ers who have found their passion and purpose in life. One area in which I have noticed a change in motivation though, since becoming a designer is in my "other" work. Self- confidence and the motivation I have experienced in my de- sign challenges me to be more "present" when I'm in my office. My relationships with my clients have become more personal and comfortable. I am allowing the "whole" me into my life, rather than compartmentalizing and distancing myself from others. In fact, this distancing technique is no longer in the equation.

I am drawn to clients and projects that align with my work ethic – and that makes it more fun! Through my success and self- confidence as a designer, I'm motivated to involve others in my work and build a team that also allows them the opportuni- ty to grow and realize their potential.

Whereas I previously delegated more operational tasks, I find that the role of motivator and coach is more productive for me as well as those around me. I trust my assistant to make the right decisions. The days of micromanaging are over for me! I have diligently pursued new techniques and obtained the necessary education and designations to further my career and expertise. I have a reputation for being enthusiastic and pride myself in getting the job right, and on time, so my client can remove that "worry" from his or her list.

The motivation to create my design business has been critical to my success. My website, AlenesAdornments.com and utilizing the potential of social media to sell my work has been ininstrumental in this process. My primary goals in life and in design are to continue challenging myself and to hold true to the passion I've come to cherish in both my art and my new life. Perhaps the perfect illustration of my motivation to continue challenging myself both in my design, as well as in my life, are my unfinished pieces. They sit waiting for me on the bench (as we jewelers refer to our workspace)! Many have been there for months, some for a couple of years. Every so often, I revisit one of these pieces and decide whether to give it more of my attention. Often the perfect vision appears and I'm inspired to finish the design, and just as often, I decide that this piece is destined for the scrap pile.

By the way, when working with metals, little is thrown out. Silver scrap may be sold for the value of the silver and much of the copper scrap is worked back into another design – and of course, gemstones can always be housed in another design. I suppose the same could be said for our journey and life in general. My biggest challenge is learning to hold true to the passion I've come to cherish.

Every experience we have, every piece of knowledge we learn can be 'stored' and used down the road. This is summed up in an experience I had at 9 years old. I was complaining to a neighbor lady about something the teacher made me study that day. Her reply; *"They can't take it away from you."* When I asked her what they can't take away, she replied, *"What you learned."*

The sum total of the creative process for me is to use the very *best* of my talents – and of me – in each piece. I am not fond of assembly line pieces and want to maintain the artisan flavor to my work. I have discovered lately that by creating my own metal designs in larger quantities, I am able to use these components and design collections of several pieces. This keeps me in the flow. I can tell if I am "in the flow" by how I feel around other jewelry designers whom I admire. If I envy their talent and experience, I know the connection is gone. When I am in the flow, I admire their designs, appreciate their talent, and feel fortunate to have made the connection, realizing that each of us brings something unique to our design aesthetic.

The Social Connection of Living Your Passion

I have several friends who are jewelry designers as well. Having this connection with those that are passionate about a similar process is so energizing. We tend to stretch each other's boundaries by sharing ideas and processes. Each of us brings our own "voice" and while I can learn much from others, my own design aesthetic is paramount to my life.

I find myself spending hours, days, and weeks creating and perfecting my designs and once the floodgates open, there is no closing them. I want to absorb every skill, every book, every technique I can get my hands on! When I'm against the wall, I require refueling by stepping away, petting my cat, spending time with my husband, going on a hike, having a glass of wine! This part of the process is enlivening and meditative all at once. The past and future does not exist for me when designing. There is only the present moment and my focus on my current project.

My Collections

My greatest, most emotional motivators are my collections. Most of my individual designs have become collections and each has special meaning to me. In the beginning of my design career, I was drawn to everything shiny, metal, and pretty!

As more of my skills developed, I began to see patterns into what resonated with me.

At times, this was as simple as absolutely loving a particular stone or shape and creating a collection around that. Other times it was about a story or event in my life that affected me personally that I wanted to recreate the feelings into a design. My collections also motivate me to express where I am in my life in general as well as in my designs, allowing me to tell my narrative and to share them with my clients.

In Section 3, I introduce you to strategies and techniques that help you move from daydreaming about accomplishing something to actually getting it done. We'll break through the various reasons for lack of motivation – you'll be surprised at how easy this will be for you – and get you back on your bench and designing with new energy or wherever your creativity takes you!

Section 3

A 5-Step Journey to Living Your Passion!

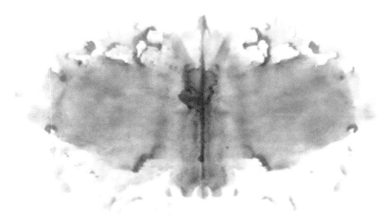

Inside the Mind of a
Jewelry Designer

A Note About the Following Exercises

I've created the following exercises to help you begin your own creative journey inward: To learn what inspires, motivates, *moves* you to create and start living your passion! Take time to thoughtfully approach these exercises; their effect can be very powerful – even life changing!

I recommend you purchase a journal in which you can record your thoughts – and remember to listen to your dreams!

Figure 8: Listen to Your Dreams

Step 1
Uncovering Your Talents

1. Discovering your calling or true desire.is not always so easy to do if you have lived a life hiding your emotions like me. Becoming our fullest selves requires some attention to what excites you. Start with things that seem simple and watch what happens. Do you get a thrill watching your baby take his or her first step, Do you love seeing the sunset or sunrise? Do mountains "fill you up" when you view them? Or is it water that feeds your soul? What about watching your cat sleep peacefully in the most comfortable spot in your house? Record in your journal your answers to the above.

2. Be aware of what moves you to smile and to feel good and then spend time appreciating these moments. The longer we spend appreciating the moment, expanding upon the joy we feel in observing these moments, the more connected we become to our complete person (our inner being if you like). These moments of extended appreciation allow us to merge our outer self (the one we present to the world) and our inner self (the one who knows our desires and capabilities). As you practice this gratitude each day, looking for more and more moments and people to

appreciate, you will feel yourself drawn to certain events, activities, people and even jobs. Allow yourself to be drawn in. Even if this event doesn't become your passion, there *is* something about the person or event that is important and leading you in the right direction. This simple process will alter your life in ways you could not have imagined. Record in your journal, when they occur, each moment of gratitude that you experienced.

3. Don't put any expectations on any of these events or people. Let it happen! I know this is easier said than done, but this is the most important part! Do not let the search to uncover your talents become another PROJECT with deadlines and expectations; it doesn't work that way!

Just go about your daily life, appreciate the special and moving moments, give them more "mind time" than just the actual event and know that you ARE in the process of discovering your true passion. Record in your journal, some of those experiences, people, things, animals you appreciate. Refer to it often and spend at least one minute re-experiencing the pleasant moments.

Step 2
Finding Your Divine Inspiration

Do you have a special place where you can totally relax and forget the world? Hiking to the top of a mountain? Lounging by the beach, appreciating the tranquility at a lake cabin? Attending Church, meditating, sitting in your garden surrounded by beauty.

Any of these experiences, and so many more, can afford you the "time off" from being in the world and provide you with the opportunity to connect to something "more." De-stressing is another word for this! To me the most important part of this is the extended time to reconnect to the inner me and disconnect from the outer façade.

I love visiting Sedona, which is a highly spiritual place. The moment we turn the corner and can see the famous red rocks and mountains, I am reenergized! Two to three days in this magical place makes everything seem right once again. What is your "Sedona"? Record it in your journal and take time to reflect on the inspiration that it provides you and how that relates to your art. Do you use those colors found in *your* "Sedona"? The shapes? The *feel* you experience when you are there? What about it *moves* you?

Step 3
Coping With Uncertainty

While some moments may seem insurmountable, the best way to handle the uncertainty of being "good enough", creating a business from your dream and moving forward daily, is to just keep going. Take the steps you need to feel comfortable with your current situation. If that involves making income in some other way, then do that. If it requires stepping back and pursuing your passion on a part time basis (like I do), then do that. None of it matters except that you DO NOT GIVE UP ON THE DREAM – the passion.

Once you have discovered what keeps you connected and brings out the best of you, then make that your primary goal each day: To feel good, to take time to get peaceful, to get away from outside influences and to have some fun! Nothing will get you back to being in the flow better than this! Having fun allows your brain to stop thinking about all the things that are not working out and allows the "inner you" to fix it! Here is an exercise that will help you cope with the uncertainty that comes up from time to time:

Sometimes a symbol can be powerfully significant, for instance, the symbols of the starfish and spiral in my collections. In this exercise, we're going to use the symbol that you choose to be a vessel of sorts, for the uncertainty that you face. Put those feelings of doubt that we all experience into the symbol to release them from inside you and unlock your power. Your first step then, is to select or make a symbol that has significance for you. Perhaps it is in nature like a seashell; perhaps it is a piece of jewelry from someone whom you loved but that is no longer with us; a symbol of strength and power. What is your symbol going to be?

1. Carry this symbol with you for the next month. Some people keep a touchstone or "lucky stone" in their pocket. Carry yours with you and acknowledge each time that you transfer your feelings of uncertainty and doubt into your symbol.

2. At the end of the month, reflect on what you have learned about yourself and your ability to release these feelings. Was it difficult? If you had to assign a number at the beginning of the month for your level of uncertainty, and one at the end, what would those numbers be? What is the reason for the improvement, i.e., a written goal, having accomplished some small tasks, etc. Record in your journal, your answers to those questions as well as the following.

3. Have you learned more about the source of your uncertainty? Is it a pattern in your life or the way you approach new

projects? How has your approach changed by transferring your uncertain and doubt into your symbol?

4.   What are you going to do with your symbol? Are you going to keep it and increase its effectiveness in helping you cope or discard it? Why? And how?

Step 4

Creating Compelling Goals

We have all heard the phrase *"working smarter, not harder."* This is especially important when deciding upon the next steps to take. Here's an exercise that can help you develop your goals – and reach them!

First, sit quietly in your favorite comfy spot with your comfort beverage (coffee for me, always.) Think about your passion: Which tasks are most fun? Most exciting? Most engaging? For me, I love the design process itself; I could play with certain components for over an hour. That's fun for me: Just thinking about how to create the piece. Record in your journal, those tasks within the process that you really enjoy, as well as your answers to the following questions:

1. Which elements are less appealing? While I enjoy most components of the process, I admit to being challenged in photographing my pieces and getting them on my website. Record the tasks within the process that you don't enjoy all that much.

2. Do you want to turn this calling into a revenue producing venture or do you want to keep this as a personal outlet for you alone while maintaining your current occupation?

3. If you could completely immerse yourself in this passionate endeavor, what would that "look" like? What would be a typical day for you? How would you arrange your schedule, etc.?

4. What are the steps necessary to make that happen? Try to start with a high-level view; you can address the details later. Keep this very general. The details will fill in later. Keeping these steps general helps you to maintain the essence of what you want. For example: A detailed step would be *'I will call 40 people to show my product.'* A more general step would be: *'I will create a list of people who might be interested.'* Again, recording your answers in your journal, helps you develop your important next steps!

Step 5

Embracing Risk to Move Forward

This is the most frightening, yet most exhilarating step! Jumping in, taking the plunge, leaping forward: Whatever you choose to call it, this is what philosophers have implied for centuries that we are *meant* to do!

The following analogy helps me cope when I am "leaping forward"! I picture myself inside a balloon, able to reach all the edges comfortably and feeling good about being connected to my boundaries (the balloon). Then I picture the risk (blowing up the balloon a little more). Now I am unsure where the boundaries/edges are. I am out of my comfort zone and moving frantically to find the new edges. But as I calm down and stretch to find the new edges, I discover more space, more opportunities and exhilaration! The following is an exercise to help you begin taking risk; be sure to record your answers in your journal.

1. Think carefully through your situation, the advantages of taking this risk and the disadvantages as well. Ask yourself *"What is the worst that can happen?"* Your answers may well be: *"I can fail. I can lose money. I could even be embarrassed."* You may realize through this process that

in the grand scheme of things, these are not such huge risks then. If you do fail, you are always free to go in a different direction and think of another way to realize your dream. The important thing is to move towards your passion – always!

2. Now record the next step if this "worse thing" does happen in order to be prepared. You'll likely learn there is another alternative, even if things don't go as you had planned. Are you ready to take the leaps? Ready to take the leap? Once you have determined that Risk and Change are all we have... then go ahead and take the plunge! If you are still uncomfortable.. just go back to step one.. relax until it feels right to redo the exercises. There is no rush. Remember: Life is about the Journey... not any particular destination.

Inside the Mind of a
Jewelry Designer

Section 4

Gallery of
My Collections

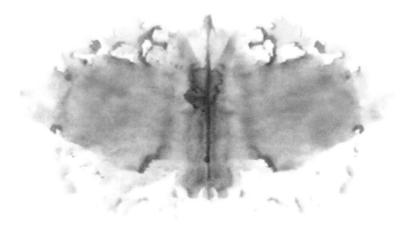

Inside the Mind of a
Jewelry Designer

11

How A Collection Is Born

Most of my designs have become collections and each has special meaning to me. In the beginning, I was drawn to everything shiny, metal and pretty. As my skills developed, I began seeing patterns into what resonated with me.

Sometimes this was as simple as absolutely loving a particular stone or design and creating a collection around that. Other times it was about a story or event in my life that affected me personally. I wanted to recreate the feelings in a design. In each of the collections that follow, I've included the a piece from my collection and the design process used for that particular piece.

Enjoy; perhaps you will find inspiration!

Inside the Mind of a
Jewelry Designer

12

Take A Risk Collection

*Do what you'd do if you knew every
dream would come true.*

"Take A Risk" is my most recent collection and the one that speaks most deeply to me. As I experimented with the process of fusing, I realized that I had no control over the outcome of the piece and, while at first this was frustrating, I saw the results and knew I had to allow them to be what *they* decided to be.

This collection reminds me of the risks I have taken in my life, as well as the times I have not, and I am inspired to take risks more often. I believe this collection offers a powerful message to everyone who wears one of these designs.

Design Process

The fusing process allows sterling silver and copper to "melt" and form its own design. Fusing always requires risk and even though I may plan a certain design, fusing creates what it wants. I love taking the risk, seeing the results and adding the finishing touches to create a truly unique piece of art. I encourage my clients to wear this piece as a reminder to take risks in their own lives!

Sterling
Earrings

Design Process

The silver back was hammered before adding the sterling scraps and the entire piece was fused until all silver was attached. Each earring, while similar is one of a kind as well!

Figure 9: Take a Risk Collection
Sterling Earrings

Antiqued Silver & Dichroic Glass Pendant

Design Process

Sterling silver and wire scraps are fused to create the design. The extreme heat creates the hole, too! I add the blue/green dichroic cabochon and antique the entire piece.

Figure 10: Take A Risk Collection
Antiqued Silver & Dichroic Glass Pendant

Copper & Sterling Free Form Pendant

Design Process

Sterling and copper are fused onto this piece and I incorporate some scrap and two interesting sterling components. I especially love the grid design in the center.

Figure 11: Take A Risk Collection
Copper & Sterling Free Form Pendant

Copper Fold Formed Pendant with Sterling & Turquoise Enhancements

Design Process

This starts as a fold formed piece of copper. I add the sterling silver components and fuse it all together. The piece just "screams" for a gem, so I add the turquoise in lower right before antiquing the entire piece.

Figure 12: Take A Risk Collection
Copper Fold Formed Pendant with Sterling & Turquoise Enhancements

Sterling Silver "Rings" with Rhodochrosite Gemstone

Design Process

I wanted to do something entirely with circles – and this is the result!   Sterling silver circles of every size and weight are fused to a sterling backing.   The center gemstone is rhodochrosite which is a stone of love.

Figure 13: Take A Risk Collection
Sterling Silver "Rings" with Rhodochrosite Gemstone

Copper & Sterling Free Form Pendant with Cubic Zirconia Gemstone

Design Process

This piece is sterling with a touch of copper and the gemstone is Cubic Zirconia, adding the glam! The entire piece is antiqued and features a sterling silver clasp and 50 deep copper colored strands.

Figure 14: Take A Risk Collection
Copper & Sterling Free Form Pendant with Cubic Zirconia Gemstone

Sterling Fold Formed Pendant

Design Process

This piece is fused sterling silver and features a beautiful opal gemstone subtly tucked in the upper left hand corner of the sterling. The strap consists of 50 strands of silver tone stainless steel finished with an oversized heavy-duty sterling silver toggle. The piece measures a full 2 inches.

Figure 15: Take A Risk Collection
Sterling Fold Formed Pendant

Inside the Mind of a
Jewelry Designer

13

Stone Soup Collection

I fell in love with these oversized slabs of gemstone that I found several years ago during the Tucson Gem Show and so, my Stone Soup Collection was born! When enhanced with sterling, pearls, leather or crystal, they become bold statements for the independent woman, reminding me of a story from childhood. I decided to create this collection based upon this story:

A hungry traveler entered a village. The villagers hoarded what little they had to eat and did not offer to share their food. Upon seeing this, the traveler filled a large iron pot with water from the nearby stream. He threw in several stones from the shore, then placed the pot in a fire ring near the edge of town. Curious villagers appeared. "What are you cooking?" they asked. "Stone Soup" he replied. "It is so delicious! Try some!" The first taster declared that it needed more flavor. He brought back a carrot from his house and placed it in the pot. One by one the villagers each added something to the pot including spices, onions, potatoes, and more, until the soup became rich and delicious – a wonderful meal for all to eat – including the traveler!

I encourage my clients to wear their necklace as a reminder that, that which we share with others will always enrich our life, as well as those around us!

Conglomerite & Forged Sterling Necklace

Design Process

I add bold hammered sterling silver links and cultured pearls to create this statement necklace. The slab is over 3" tall!

Figure 16: Stone Soup Collection
Conglomerite & Forged Sterling Necklace

Brioche Agate & Sterling Necklace

Design Process

This variety of agate features multiple colored browns, tans and car-amels. I add a simple sterling silver chain to enhance the stone.

Figure 17: Stone Soup Collection
Brioche Agate & Sterling Necklace

Brioche Agate (All Stones) Necklace

Design Process

This particular slab tends more to the darker brown tones, so I add more stone to *really* enhance the slab.

Figure 18: Stone Soup Collection
Brioche Agate (All Stones)

Onyx & Leather Necklace

Design Process

This 2 ½" tall stone slab features the natural stone. Onyx rarely occurs as solid black and in this case, the white veins create a lovely, one of a kind feature. An oversized clasp and black leather add the finishing touches.

Figure 19: Stone Soup Collection
Onyx & Leather Necklace

Serpentine & Leather Necklace

Design Process

Rich Lime green Serpentine features veins of darker green creating this striking combination. I added sterling silver, serpentine stone chips and black leather to create the necklace design.

Figure 20: Stone Soup Collection
Serpentine & Leather Necklace

Onyx, Sterling & Gems Necklace

Design Process

Natural onyx is often very light brown tending to gold tones. This slab shows off many of these colors and is enhanced with natural onyx round beads.

Figure 21: Stone Soup Collection
Onyx, Sterling & Gems Necklace

14

Copper Cuff Collection

Each of the copper cuffs and rings are treated to maintain the patinas I have created. This treatment also prevents further oxidation and "greening" of your wrist or finger.

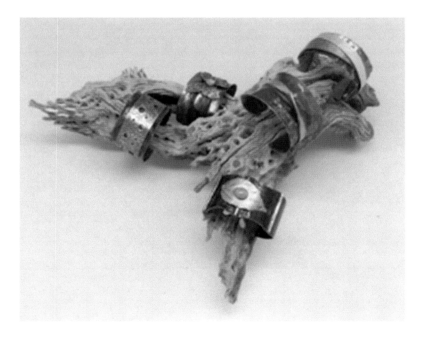

**Figure 22: Southwest Spirit, Be Transformed, Desert Sands,
Metal in Motion, Sonoran Sky**

Fold Formed & Peanut Oil Copper Cuff

Design Process

Raw copper is heated to soften the metal (called annealing). I place the fold in the center and then twist it to create the gentle fold from side to side. The patina is more heat and peanut oil.

Figure 23: Copper Cuff Collection
Desert Sands Copper Form Folded Cuff

Formed, Sterling & Turquoise Copper Cuff

Design Process

Form folds are created first, then the blue/green patina is created with vinegar and ammonia. Sterling silver is riveted to the center and the greenish turquoise gemstone is soldered to the center of the silver.

Figure 24: Copper Cuff Collection
Saguaro Landscape Formed, Sterling & Turquoise Copper Cuff

Formed, Sterling & Charoite Copper Cuff

Design Process

Pure copper is form folded and then treated with heat to create the finish. Sterling silver is hammered (called forging) to create the texture. The center gemstone is Charoite from Russia.

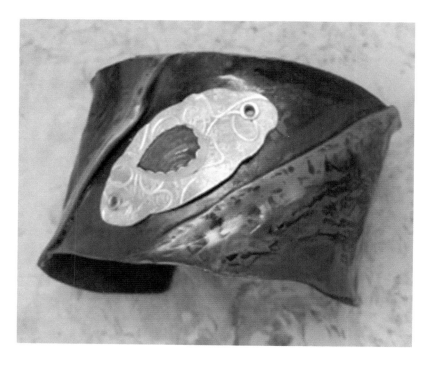

Figure 25: Copper Cuff Collection
Lavender Splendor Formed, Sterling & Charoite Copper Cuff

Accordion Formed, Sterling & Brass
Copper Cuff

Design Process

The accordion design is achieved by creating multiple folds (I apply heat to soften after each fold). A strip of sterling and a strip of brass are forged to create texture and then riveted to the cuff.

Figure 26: Copper Cuff Collection
Accordion Formed, Sterling & Brass Copper Cuff

Butterfly & Turquoise Copper Cuff

Design Process

Copper is form folded and a vinegar /ammonia patina creates the blue finish. The butterfly is sterling silver that has been forged and antiqued before adding the turquoise gemstone.

Figure 27: Copper Cuff Collection
Transformation Butterfly & Turquoise Copper Cuff

15

Sacred Spiral Collection

The spiral, starting as a smaller, tight circle, is found in cave carvings, shells, the Milky Way and even in the double helix structure of our DNA and is an ancient symbol representing growth and evolution. Each of our actions – a quick smile to a stranger, holding the door for someone, a kind word to a friend – seem like small gestures. But the resulting ripples of joy they cause, like the circles in a spiral, are infinite and precious to another.

Design Process

During one of my jewelry metal classes, the instructor showed us how to create spiral baskets of sterling to house gemstones. I loved the process and used it in my earlier designs. One day as I was playing around with the sterling, I discovered that if I left the basket in its flat position instead of opening it up, I had a perfect double spiral. I love the concept of the spiral going to infinity, so another collection was born!

Red Creek and Sterling Sacred Spiral Necklace

Design Process

Red Creek Jasper is named for the stream that runs through the area of China where it was discovered and features rich reds, browns and blacks. For the piece below, sterling silver is shaped, textured and forged into a spiral.

Figure 28: Sacred Spiral Collection
Red Creek and Sterling Sacred Spiral Necklace

Copper & Fused Sterling Ring

Design Process

Pure copper is textured before fusing the sterling silver spirals to the surface. The ring is then shaped and I add heat to create the rustic finish.

Figure 29: Sacred Spiral Collection
Copper & Fused Silver Ring

Fold Formed, Fused Ring

Design Process

Fold formed copper is created by heating and folding the copper. I fuse the sterling silver spiral into the copper before final shaping.

Figure 30: Sacred Spiral Collection
Fold Formed, Fused Ring

Sterling & Amethyst Necklace

Design Process

Each of the strands is created with amethyst nougats and stones, keeping the signature sterling silver spiral featured prominently.

Figure 31: Sacred Spiral Collection
Sterling & Amethyst Necklace

Copper, Fused Sterling Earrings

Design Process

Pure copper is textured before fusing the sterling silver spirals and chips. I use heat and borax to create the patina for the copper.

Figure 32: Sacred Spiral Collection
Copper, Fused Sterling Earrings

16

Akonye Kena Collection

Translated as "I Will Help Myself"

Last year during the Tucson Gem Show I encountered a supplier offering an unusual looking bead collection. I discovered that these were recycled beads made from used magazines and were incredibly lightweight – this intrigued me – then I discovered that these beads were created as part of a sustainability project in Northern Uganda and I was hooked!

This bead product line started as an exercise within a rehabilitation program. Rolling beads was intended to train young women from the streets in discipline and attention to detail and has since expanded into the primary source of income for the project. The proceeds provide a living with fair wage for them. Akonye Kena promotes independence and self-sufficiency initiatives in East Africa.

My collection features these recycled beads along with pearls, sterling, copper and gemstones.

Sterling and Polymer Bracelet

Design Process

Recycled magazines are used to create the rich green beads. Colorful polymer clay focal beads add deep purples to complement the recycled beads. I create the sterling silver twists by opening up my spiral sterling silver design.

Figure 33: Akonye Kena Collection
Sterling and Polymer Bracelet

Copper, Mother of Pearl Bracelet

Design Process

This particular bracelet was created using the multi colored blue and magenta Akonye Kena beads. Unusually shaped Mother of Pearl beads were just begging to be part of this design! I used copper for the metal since it brings out the colors of the beads so nicely.

Figure 34: Akonye Kena Collection
Copper, Mother of Pearl Bracelet

Copper, Swarovski Crystal Earrings

Design Process

These diamond shaped Akonye Kena beads feature many tones of brown, tan and even black. They are the perfect complement for teardrop shaped Swarovski crystals and pure copper.

Figure 35: Akonye Kena Collection
Copper, Swarovski Crystal Earrings

Copper Disc Earrings

Design Process

These deep blue Akonye Kena beads are bulb shaped. This shape meshes perfectly with my pure copper discs to create a perfect shorter earring length for those who prefer that style.

Figure 36: Akonye Kena Collection
Copper Discs Earrings

Sterling & Onyx Earrings

Design Process

Akonye Kena diamond shaped green beads with black accents are elegant in design to which I add sterling silver and
black onyx gemstones.

Figure 37: Akonye Kena Collection
Sterling & Onyx Earrings

17

Pure Metal Collection

This collection was requested by several of my clients who loved their copper cuff bracelet and wanted earrings to complement them. I love working with metal, so it would seem appropriate that a Pure Metal Collection would ensue! I have incorporated the use of sterling silver, copper, and brass in these designs. Each is still one-of-a-kind, although I am in the process of developing two designs that will have multiple copies.

Why is metal so much fun? I can harden it, soften it, add texture, add patterns, shape it and patina it in so many different ways! Starting with pure metal sheet (or sometimes wire) I can create just about any look I desire.

Design Process

In creating the Pure Metal Collection, once the hammering, texturing, shaping and forming are done, I add one of several patinas. My favorite patinas are:

- Vinegar and ammonia to create a blue-green color on copper and brass;

- Peanut oil and heat to darken the copper and give it a rich brown- black tint
- Plain old heat to give copper a reddish tone; and
- Liver of sulfur (the only one that works on Sterling) to blacken the piece; then I shine up the areas I want to highlight.

Copper and Dichroic Glass Pendant

Design Process

Copper is formed in the shape of a leaf to which I add texture
through forging and the piece de resistance – a gorgeous dichroic glass cabochon.   This reminds me so much of the
ambers and oranges in our Arizona Sunset!

Figure 38: Pure Metal Collection
Sonoran Sunset Copper & Dichroic Glass Pendant

Pure Copper & Antiquated Silver Earrings

Design Process

Copper is textured with a subtle design, then shaped and finished with a heat patina. The sterling silver texture is bolder and antiqued to highlight the design.

Figure 39: Pure Metal Collection
Pure Copper & Antiquated Silver Earrings

Copper with Blue Patina and Antiqued Copper Accents Earrings

Design Process

Pure Copper is formed and textured and then I add the vinegar/ammonia patina to create the blue/green color. The smaller copper discs are textured and antiqued with liver of sulfur.

Figure 40: Pure Metal Collection
Copper with Blue Patina and Antiqued Copper Accents Earrings

Copper, Sterling & Amethyst Nougat Earrings

Design Process

I begin with a pure copper sheet and saw out the triangle design. Then I use a hole punch in the center. The copper is forged and hammered first, then the patina is created with peanut oil and heat. I add the gorgeous amethyst gemstone nougats and sterling silver links as the finishing touch!

Figure 41: Pure Metal Collection
Copper, Sterling & Amethyst Nougat Earrings

Copper Disc Earrings with Antiqued Sterling Silver Accent

Design Process

This copper is formed and die cut for the open and airy look. The sterling silver discs feature a different texture and antiqued finish.

Figure 42: Pure Metal Collection
Copper Disc Earrings with Antiqued Sterling Silver Accent

Dendritic Agate, Copper and Sterling Dust Earrings

Design Process

Copper is scalloped and sterling silver "dust" is fused right into the copper. This process combined with the heat patina creates a reddish tint with glints of sparkling silver. The gemstone is a heart shaped Dendritic agate.

Figure 43: Pure Metal Collection
Dendritic Agate, Copper and Sterling Dust Earrings

Copper and Sterling "Peanut Oil" Earrings

Design Process

Starting with a copper sheet, I saw out the rounded square design and then hole punch the center creating the open look I want to achieve. The sterling silver free form shapes are forged and hammered before cutting. A patina of peanut oil and heat creates the deep tones in the copper.

Figure 44: Pure Metal Collection
Copper and Sterling 'Peanut Oil' Earrings

Inside the Mind of a
Jewelry Designer

18

Starfish Collection

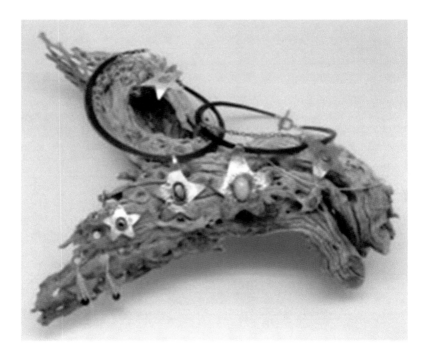

**Figure 45: Sterling and Australian Opal Starfish Pendant,
Pure Copper & Malachite Gemstone Pendant, Antiqued Sterling Silver & Tur-
quoise, Gemstone Pendant, Sterling Silver & Picture Jasper Starfish Necklace,
Bright Hammered Copper, Sterling & Malachite Starfish Earrings**

My Starfish Collection, introduced a few years ago, resonates deeply within my clients and me. Initially, I added gems to glass starfish that I purchased to enhance the necklace, however now I create my own starfish from sterling or copper. Each time I create one of these, I recall the following story:

A man was walking towards the water's edge early one morning and noticed a small boy running along the beach. The boy was picking up starfish that had washed up on shore and throwing them into the water. As there were hundreds of starfish and only one small boy, the man was struck by the futility of his task. He yelled to the boy, "Why are you wasting your time picking up the starfish?! You cannot save all these starfish!"

The boy looked at the man, and then at the starfish he had in his hand. He threw the starfish into the water and said, "Maybe I can't save them all, but I sure made a difference to that one!"

Who can you make a difference to today?

Sterling and Australian Opal Starfish Pendant

Design Process

Pure sterling silver is hammered (forged) to create the texture. The Australian opal gemstone is luminous and multi colored as it reflects the light.

Figure 46: Starfish Collection
Sterling and Australian Opal Starfish Pendant

Pure Copper and Malachite
Gemstone Starfish Pendant

Design Process

A copper sheet is shaped and textured to create the starfish and then I solder the copper bezel to the backing and insert this rich green malachite gemstone.

Figure 47: Starfish Collection
Pure Copper and Malachite Gemstone Starfish Pendant

Bright Hammered Copper, Sterling & Malachite Starfish Earrings

Design Process

Copper is hammered to create the texture. I keep the original bright copper finish so they will contrast against the deep green malachite beads and sterling silver links.

Figure 48: Starfish Collection
Bright Hammered Copper, Sterling & Malachite Starfish Earrings

Antiqued Sterling Silver and Turquoise Gemstone Starfish Pendant

Design Process

This sterling silver starfish is cut from silver sheet. I form the sterling and add an antiqued finish to bring out the texture. The baby blue turquoise gemstone completes the design.

Figure 49: Starfish Collection
Antiqued Sterling Silver and Turquoise Gemstone Starfish Pendant

Sterling Silver & Picture Jasper
Starfish Necklace

Design Process

I enhance this overall look by adding picture jasper gemstones throughout the entire necklace. This gemstone is called picture jasper because it is so easy to see landscapes in the indi-individual pieces.

Figure 50: Starfish Collection
Sterling Silver & Picture Jasper Starfish Necklace

Inside the Mind of a
Jewelry Designer

19

Gemstone Myths

Gemstones are truly inspiring, not only in their beauty but also in the mythology that surrounds them and the powers that they bestow on the wearer. I research the mythology and history of the stones as I incorporate these amazing gems into my work and include a Romance Card with each piece.

In this section, I share an overview of these myths along with a piece that I have designed to show their beauty within a finished design. Below are some of the fascinating myths; for more details on each gemstone, please visit my website, AlenesAdornments.com to read my individual blog posts.

Agate

Agate is a semiprecious variety of quartz. The gems form in cavities of lavas or rocks and are characterized either by color bands or moss-like inclusions. It is believed that Agate enhances mental function, improving concentration and perception. My design below features a rich and earthy Brioche Agate stone slab measuring a full 2" tall. The strap consists of three strands of light and dark brown leather with silver clasp and components. As you can see, this gem makes a true statement!

Figure 51: Brioche Agate & Leather Necklace

Amethyst

Amethyst, a variety of quartz, is found mainly in Brazil and Uruguay. Ancient Greeks believed that drinking wine from a cup made from this gem would make them immune to intoxication! Amethyst is believed to calm the mind and help the wearer feel less scattered.

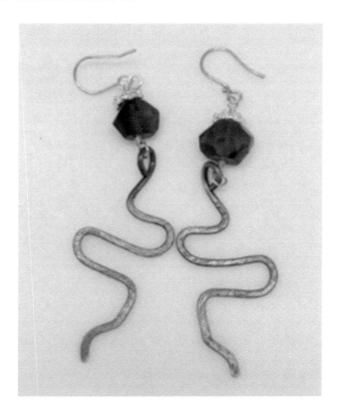

Figure 52: Amethyst Gemstone Nougat Earrings

Amazonite

Amazonite is a blue/green mineral named after the Amazon River. It is believed that Amazonite absorbs microwave and cell phone emanations and its soothing properties calm the brain and nervous system while alleviating worry and fear.

My design below features a rich aqua blue Amazonite gemstone enhanced by gray-black inclusions. You'll note that the delicate dangle sterling links are heart shaped!

Figure 53: Amazonite & Sterling Earrings

Cultured Pearl

A pearl is formed when an irritant is implanted into the pearl sack of the mollusk, which then secretes layers of nacre to protect itself from the irritant. These layers create the pearl!

My design below features Mother of Pearl, pure copper and multicolored beads made from recycled magazines. The Mother of Pearl is a perfect complement for the Akonye Kena beads and toggle clasp.

Figure 54: Cultured Coin Pearls and Hammered Brass Earrings

Fire Agate

Agate is a variety of quartz. Fire Agate has inclusions of reddish to brown hematite that give an internal iridescence to the stones, which is believed to aid relaxation and enhance meditation through its calming effect on the body.

My design below features vibrant Orange Fire Agate faceted gemstones as the focal point of this design. Twist beach and sterling silver are the perfect complement for this gorgeous gemstone.

Figure 55: Fire Agate & Sterling Silver Bracelet

Hematite

Hematite is a dense iron oxide, made of 70 percent iron. The word hematite is derived from the Greek 'Haimatitis' meaning 'blood-red' which is the color of the powder form of the mineral. Hematite is believed to dissolve negativity and prevent negative energies from entering the aura. Hematite amulets have been found in nearly every Pharaoh's tomb as a support in the afterlife.

My design below features brilliant, silver-black Hematite and open cut sterling silver to create the Wow Factor in this bracelet!

Figure 56: Hematite & Open Cut Antiqued Sterling Silver Bracelet

Jade

Jade or Jadeite is a mineral available in a wide range of colors including white (in its purest form), green, lilac, pink, brown, red, blue, black, orange and yellow. Jade is a symbol of purity and serenity; Golden Jade is energetic.

My design below features silver shaped into open circles with the golden jade dangling below and deep green jade chips, adding wonderful contrast.

Figure 57: Green and Golden Jade Sterling Earrings

Jasper

Jasper is a dense variety of quartz. Colors vary depending upon the inclusions with many appearing to have images on them. Babylonians considered Jasper a female stone as it is believed that, when it's worn, it relieves birth pains. Vibrant Picture Jasper is so named because the inclusions appear to form pictures like mountain ranges – beautiful! I use a designer sterling silver bezel to encase the gemstone and a sterling silver arched bail that adds to the overall design. The necklace contains 50 strands of coated stainless steel and features an oversized toggle clasp in sterling silver.

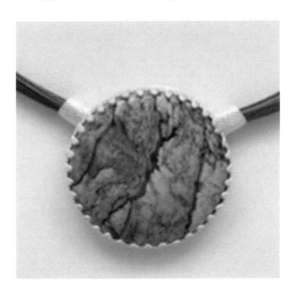

Figure 58: Picture Jasper & Sterling Necklace

Onyx

Onyx is a semiprecious variety of agate found primarily in Italy, Mexico, and Russia and believed to provide strength, steadfastness, and stamina to those who wear it.

My design below is from my Sacred Spiral Collection and features banded Onyx gemstones, sterling silver links, and Swarovski Crystals surrounding the spirals for which the design is named. The oversized Lobster clasp allows for ease of use.

Figure 59: Onyx & Sterling Sacred Spiral Necklace

Rhodochrosite

Rhodochrosite is also known as the Inca Rose since ancient Natives of the Andes believed it contained blood from ancestral great rulers. This gemstone is said to contain love energy and aid in the wearer's emotional healing. Rhodochrosite is associated with the heart chakra.

My design below features rhodochrosite within a pure copper sheet, fold formed and heat-treated to create the cuff. The name of my piece, *Love In Bloom*, perfectly describes the sterling silver leaf design and center stone of rhodochrosite!

Figure 60: Love in Bloom Pure Copper, Sterling & Rhodochrosite Cuff Bracelet

Serpentine

The apple green variety of Serpentine is also known as Yellow Turquoise or "Noble Serpentine." Serpentine is a silicate mineral rich in magnesium and is mined in England, Canada, China, and the US. Serpentine is believed to promote compassion and to clear emotional baggage from previous relationships.

My design below features a piece from my *Take A Risk Collection* and features apple green Serpentine, complimented by Mother of Pearl and sterling silver. Once the design itself is created, I add the antiqued finish and arch the pendant slightly. Note the spiral at the edge of the pendant too! Also featured are an oversized toggle clasp and sterling silver links.

Figure 61: Sterling & Serpentine Necklace

Sodalite

Sodalite, named for its high sodium content, is found primarily in Maine, New Hampshire, Arkansas, Russia, and Germany. It is believed that sodalite helps eliminate mental confusion and encourage rational thought.

My design below features a piece from my *Stone Soup Collection*; a stunning blue Sodalite stone slab measuring a full 3¼" tall! Pearl and sterling silver links complete the design. This is a real show stopper!

Figure 62: Sodalite Slab Necklace

Tiger Eye

Tiger Eye is a variety of quartz, traditionally considered a protective stone and worn as a talisman; best known for the light band that resembles a tiger's eye. When worn this stone promotes clarity and integrity.

My design below features Tiger Eye gemstone bezel set in silver atop a pure copper cuff, which is fold formed several times to create an accordion effect. Heat is applied in between each folding, then the finish is created using a patina of heat. Finally, I hammer the sterling silver to introduce a new texture into the design. The title of the piece, *Desert Radiance*, describes the brilliant hues of browns and caramel found in cuff and the Tiger Eye.

Figure 63: *Desert Radiance* **Copper, Sterling &
Tiger Eye Cuff Bracelet**

Turquoise

Turquoise beads date as far back as 5000 BC having been found in Mesopotamia. Turquoise, considered a purification stone, is said to dispel negative energy and align the chakras when worn.

My design below features a focal piece of a stunning green turquoise gemstone atop pure copper which has been fold formed and forged prior to adding the gorgeous green patina (created by combining vinegar and ammonia).

**Figure 64: Arizona Turquoise Gemstone with
Sterling and Copper Cuff**

List of Figures

16186754R00088

Made in the USA
Charleston, SC
08 December 2012